All Time Favorite
GERSHWIN™ CLASSICS

CONTENTS

BUT NOT FOR ME

Words and Music by
GEORGE GERSHWIN
and IRA GERSHWIN

6

molto rit.

8va ⅃

THE MAN I LOVE

Music and Lyrics by
GEORGE GERSHWIN
and IRA GERSHWIN

SOON

Music and Lyrics by
GEORGE GERSHWIN
and IRA GERSHWIN

Moderate Rhumba rhythm

molto rit.

mf lightly

BIDIN' MY TIME

Music and Lyrics by
GEORGE GERSHWIN
and IRA GERSHWIN

18

(semi-staccato touch in L.H.)

legato gradual cresc. to end

8va

CLAP YO' HANDS

Music and Lyrics by
GEORGE GERSHWIN
and IRA GERSHWIN

With spirit, a la polonaise

HE LOVES AND SHE LOVES

Music and Lyrics by
GEORGE GERSHWIN
and IRA GERSHWIN

A little faster

rit.

Broadly

SWANEE

Words by
IRVING CAESAR

Music by
GEORGE GERSHWIN

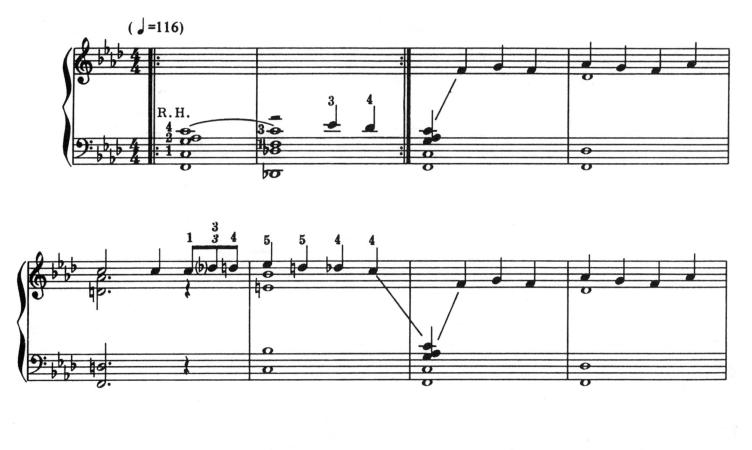

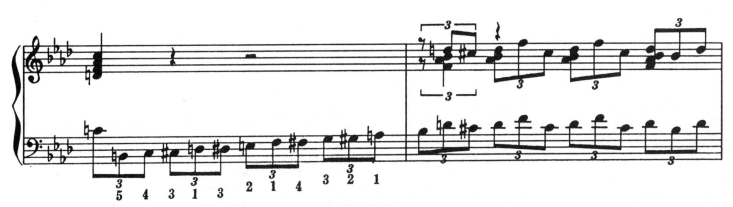

STRIKE UP THE BAND

Music and Lyrics by
GEORGE GERSHWIN
and IRA GERSHWIN

Brightly

SOMEONE TO WATCH OVER ME

Music and Lyrics by
GEORGE GERSHWIN
and IRA GERSHWIN

chorus repeat

I'm a little lamb

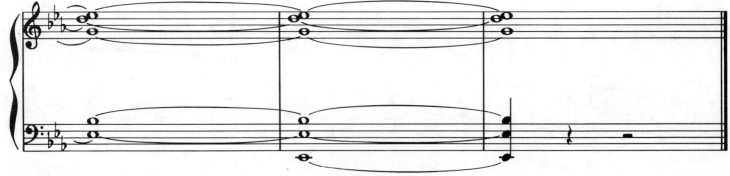

I'LL BUILD A STAIRWAY TO PARADISE

Words by
B.G. DeSYLVA and IRA GERSHWIN

Music by
GEORGE GERSHWIN

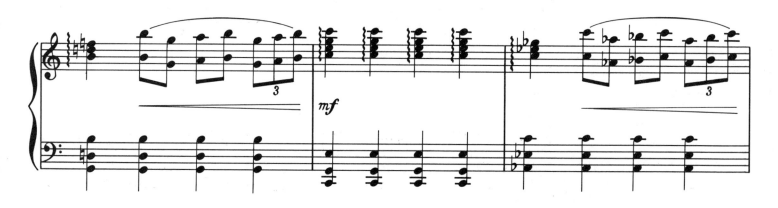

EMBRACEABLE YOU

Music and Lyrics by
GEORGE GERSHWIN
and IRA GERSHWIN

Moderately slow (♩=84)

55

HOW LONG HAS THIS BEEN GOING ON?

Music and Lyrics by
GEORGE GERSHWIN
and IRA GERSHWIN

Moderate Blues

SOMEBODY LOVES ME

Words by
B.G. DeSYLVA
and BALLARD MACDONALD

Music by
GEORGE GERSHWIN

FASCINATING RHYTHM

Music and Lyrics by
GEORGE GERSHWIN
and IRA GERSHWIN

Driving "Stride" Boogie beat

Fast, with an even rhythm (♪♪ = ♪♪)

Presto, with abandon

'S WONDERFUL

Music and Lyrics by
GEORGE GERSHWIN
and IRA GERSHWIN

MAYBE

Music and Lyrics by
GEORGE GERSHWIN and
and IRA GERSHWIN

Moderately

LOVE IS SWEEPING THE COUNTRY

Music and Lyrics by
GEORGE GERSHWIN
and IRA GERSHWIN

Brightly

8va
8va
8va
loco

LIZA
(ALL THE CLOUDS'LL ROLL AWAY)

Words by
IRA GERSHWIN and GUS KAHN

Music by
GEORGE GERSHWIN

Delicate "Waltz" tempo

I GOT RHYTHM

Music and Lyrics by
GEORGE GERSHWIN
and IRA GERSHWIN

92

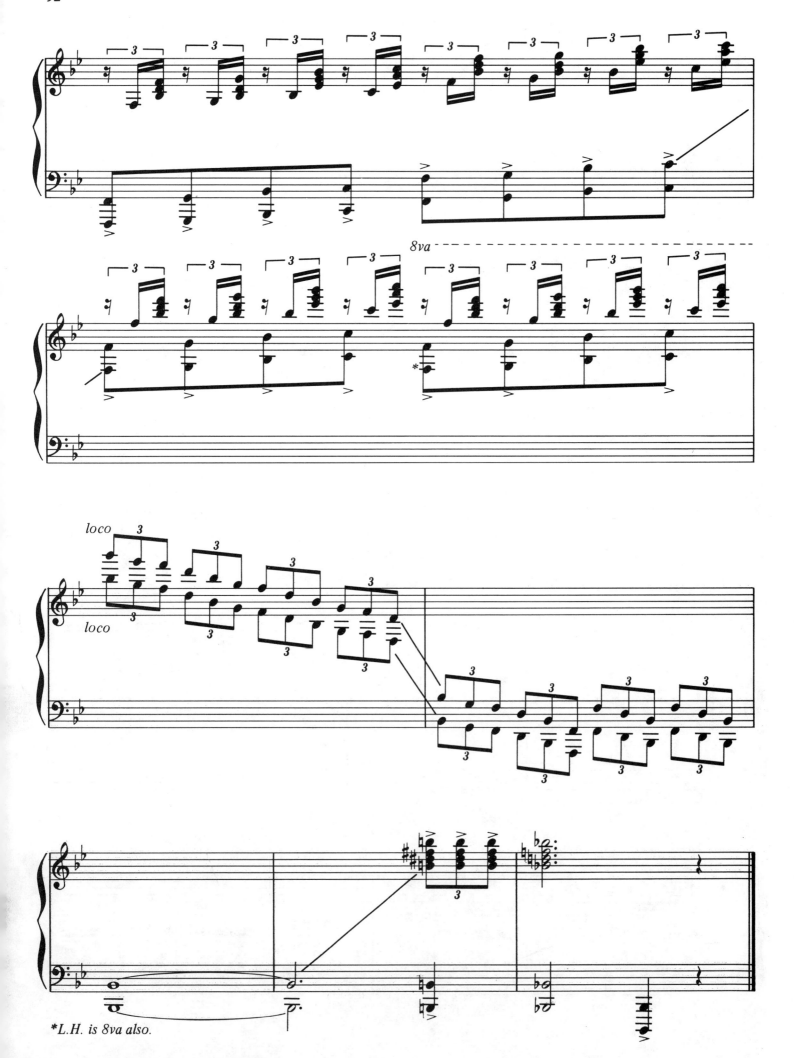

*L.H. is 8va also.

I'VE GOT A CRUSH ON YOU

Music and Lyrics by
GEORGE GERSHWIN
and IRA GERSHWIN

Allegretto giocoso

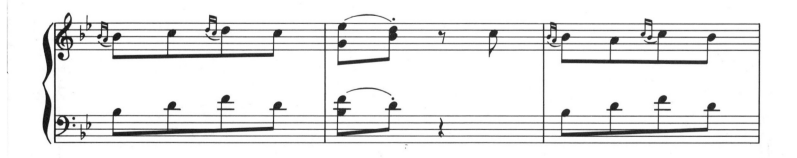

94

Slowly and sustained

L.H.

R.H.

L.H.
with pedal throughout

rit.

* *The melody (top note of roll) should be played by cross over L.H.*